UNVEILED FACES

Cherish Bickel

And we all, who with unveiled faces contemplate the Lord's glory, are being transformed into his image with ever-increasing glory, which comes from the Lord, who is the Spirit.

2 Corinthians 3:18

CONTENTS

CONTENTS

ABOUT THE COVER

As I flew over the Tonle Sap River to Phnom Penh, Cambodia, I looked down at the landscape below. The sun shone down on the land, casting golden hues along the water while the nutrient-rich soil shone with deep purple undertones. As beautiful as this view was, it was skewed only by the beaten-up window of the old ATR 72 propeller plane; years of abuse, scratches, and untouched dirt had built up a veil of distortion.

Immediately, I realized that this veil did not prevent anyone from seeing Cambodia's glory below, but it hampered one from seeing its fullness. Just so, we can all behold God and His glory, but to view Him unveiled, healed of the abuses and trauma of life, we see more of the fullness of His beauty. As we gaze on Him and His glory, we receive, like a mirror, the perfect image of Him and become transformed into His image.

As we choose to heal from our past hurts and pains, we are able to see more clearly the fullness of God the Father's perfect love and see Him in others. This beautiful, unskewed view burns a deeper passion for Him to be revealed to all with unveiled faces.

May we all be transformed from glory to glory.

INTRODUCTION

Dear Follower of Christ,

I am so happy you picked up this book! It is my hope that this book can help bridge the gap between deliverance and emotional healing. It is my desire to give individuals the tools they need to find further healing and freedom by partnering with the Father and the truth of His word.

This book will not cover the Biblical basis or go in-depth on the 'how' or 'why' of emotional healing?; there are many books for that. This book, however, is meant to be a quick, easy-to-use tool with simple steps for those who know that Truth can set them free. This book would best be used in partnership with deliverance, either after an in-person deliverance or after going through a self-deliverance manual such as *The Self Deliverance Guide* by Mike Brewer.

I firmly believe that each Believer carries the authority to cast out demons, even from themselves, and the ability to partner with God to receive further levels of healing and breakthrough while tearing down strongholds. This is because much of my freedom was found in this manner: first, through knowing the tools to find emotional healing, then through following a self-deliverance guide. Doing in-person sessions is a wonderful thing that is not to be discounted, but knowing how to use the tools for yourself is invaluable and more easily reproducible. He is coming back for a spotless Bride, and I am so thankful that the Body is welcoming the power of deliverance back into the Church (where it was until the mid-1700s)!

My hope with this book is that you will be equipped:

- First, to hear the voice of God
- Second, to identify the roots of negative thoughts and emotions while partnering with Holy Spirit.
- Third, how to continually renew your mind.

You will learn all of this in the first three chapters! The following chapters are to help give tools for recognizing and uprooting specific thoughts, behaviors, and mindsets. You are welcome to read through each chapter consecutively or jump to the one you need the most after you have learned the tools given in Chapters One through Three.

This book is not meant to take the place of training for emotional healing ministry. There is much to be taken into account when it comes to using these tools on others, and in-person training with mentorship is highly recommended before stepping into that.

I hope this book blesses you and takes you deeper into ever-increasing glory, all by the power of God.

Blessings,
Cherish

We demolish arguments and every pretension that sets itself up against the knowledge of God, and we take captive every thought to make it obedient to Christ.
2 Corinthians 10:5 NIV

Do not conform to the pattern of this world, but be transformed by the renewing of your mind. Then you will be able to test and approve what God's will is—his good, pleasing and perfect will.
Romans 12:2 NIV

◆ ◆ ◆

1. HEARING FROM GOD

I will stand at my watch
  and station myself on the ramparts;
I will look to see what he will say to me,
  and what answer I am to give to this complaint.
Habakkuk 2:1 NIV

Deliverance and emotional healing are having a resurgence in the Church today, and it is something to be greatly excited about! These two elements of freedom that Christ made available to all are life-changing as people are set free from the bondage of the flesh and are filled all the more with the Holy Spirit.

Many churches are moving powerfully in these areas, but there are many more people that are hungry to be equipped. Countless individuals desire freedom but do not know where they can go to get it. It is for that reason that several have made deliverance guides that can be done at home to break curses off of the bloodlines and expel demons. However, there seems to be a gap that needs to be filled. While the tools for deliverance from home have been given out, the aftercare and breaking down of strongholds has been nearly left untapped. I want to partner with that freedom others have brought to teach you to break down the stronghold of the mind, finding emotional healing in the process. I believe in this process because it is one I have walked through and found tremendous healing.

There are three primary keys you need to walk out emotional healing on your own:

- First is faith that God is good and desires to see you healed and free.

- Second is the ability to hear from God for yourself. Don't fret, learning how to hear Him is simple!

- Third, you need to be free from demonic influences that could try to manipulate your thoughts. The processes in this book can be done while taking steps to freedom but it is meant to be partnered with deliverance.

All believers can hear from God. Often the hard part is recognizing that He is communicating with us. There are 7 primary ways that people hear from Him:

1. Audibly
2. Internal hearing
3. Knowing/drop in the spirit
4. Sensing
5. Visions
6. Images in the mind
7. Dreams

Once a person recognizes the way they hear from God, they often remember where He had been speaking to them long ago. Many people will hear from Him in more than one way, but often have a primary way. I have been fortunate to hear from God in each of these seven ways though most commonly I hear Him internally or with a knowing.

Another hurdle that some face is the fear of saying that God spoke to them. This is placed on people by false religious restrictions and fear of man. There is a weightiness to admitting that God spoke and a desire to be accurate that is healthy, but there is a fear of admitting it that is unhealthy. Distinguishing between the two is important in order to move forward in confidence knowing that God desires intimacy with His children and that intimacy requires communication.

The voice of God is often a still small voice that draws us to Him and leads us in direction. Let's break the ways of hearing down a little, shall we?

Audibly

Most people want to hear from God audibly, but this is the least common way to hear from Him. Most people who have heard His audible voice (with their outer ear), have only heard it once or maybe a few times. Many people stumble on this because they expect this is the way they will hear. It is generally easy to know when God has spoken audibly and hard to deny it.

As a child I experienced God speaking "from the other room" one time which took me years to recognize as the audible voice of God. I had dealt with horrific nightmares every night for as long as I could remember. I prayed for them to go away every night. One day, as I sat on top of my bunk bed, I heard a man's deep voice from the other room which seemed like a radio had been turned on.

As clear as day, the voice said, "You have been given authority. You can command even bad dreams to go away in the name of Jesus and they will stop." This simple instruction that even the heart of a child could grasp hit my spirit and I rose up in authority that day against the fear that attacked me each night. Whenever a bad dream would start, I would command it to end and from that point on I rarely experienced a nightmare again. On the few occasions I did, I took authority over it and even began to have the demons behind the dreams reveal their true identity and root causes, which I was then able to work through healing and gain freedom from.

Another instance where I heard God's audible voice was after I had ignored His voice for days despite Him warned me that someone was in imminent danger. I kept insisting that it was my mind making things up. Finally, one night He got my attention audibly and urgently. It was terrifying, honestly. I jumped to attention and ran to obey. I had no way of knowing the life-saving measures that would be taking place that day. That person lives a beautiful healthy life now and I cannot imagine the devastation that would have come if He had not graciously shaken me with His audible voice, even after I ignored Him for so long. This brings me to how many hear His voice, internally.

Internal Hearing

Based on conversations with others, this and "knowing" are the most common ways people hear from the Father. This type of hearing is often thought to be our own thoughts or even our conscience. It is an inner dialogue with the still small voice of God guiding, instructing, and encouraging.

As I mentioned, I have ignored His voice many times by crediting it to my own thoughts. I have seen the fruit of listening and the devastation of ignoring it when assuming I was overimagining.

The day before we found out our fifth child was a boy, I heard the voice of God internally declare that our son's name was to be Nehemiah, followed by a prophetic word about his life and a season for our family. My response was less than graceful as I was certain we were having a girl! Fifteen hours later, the ultrasound tech declared that we were, in fact, having a boy.

In another instance, I was taking my husband to the dentist for an emergency treatment. I repeatedly heard in my head, "Turn around! Go home!" I argued that I couldn't, my husband had already missed too much work and was in immense pain, so we had no choice but to go. "Turn around! Go home." I tried to convince myself that it was a strange bout of anxiety due to driving in the rain. "Turn around! Go home," but I kept driving. Moments later, I came upon an eighteen-wheeler that was stopped below a bridge. It is a low-lying bridge where the road has a dip and drivers often get nervous wondering if the maximum height listed could be correct. I stopped behind him, and the white car behind me stopped as well. Behind them was a flatbed truck whose driver was on his phone texting. He did not see the line of cars at a stop and swerved just in time to miss the car behind me, but he lost control in the process. The back of his flatbed swung around and hit into the back of my fairly new minivan, totaling the vehicle. He then fled the scene, dragging his trailer down the side of my van in the process.

I had four young children in the car who, by the grace of God, were protected that day! Our daughter who was sitting where the flatbed came into the vehicle had brought along a big fluffy blanket on that hot August day. She was burrowed down low in her seat completely covered when the glass exploded over her. Everyone and everything, including our six-month-old, was covered in glass, but everyone was okay. From that day on, I have known how immensely important it is to not ignore that still-small voice that guides and instructs us for our well-being.

His voice was a quiet nudging that was easy to confuse with my own thoughts. When you align your life with Him, your thoughts begin to look like His thoughts. That simple "nudging of the Holy Spirit" is God speaking to you. Often we may hear people say something along the lines of "I felt like I was supposed to give this stranger $100, and when I did they broke down and told me how they needed that exact amount." Or, "John was on my mind all morning so I called him and it saved his life." These aren't extreme examples, they are ones I have heard over and over. This is the internal hearing of the Holy Spirit! Once we recognize this we can lean in and listen a little closer to what He has to say.

Knowing & Sensing

For a long time I was a "knower". I couldn't explain why I knew or how I knew what I knew, I just knew it. In all honesty, it was frustrating at times and caused a few riffs between my husband and I. I would be certain that I knew something without a doubt, and he would just want to know how I knew it. It didn't help that I was not aware at the time that this is one way that God speaks to His children. Some people may refer to this as "it just dropped in their spirit." There is no thought, no voice, no dialogue, it is as if the information is just downloaded into them.

Those who hear by knowing can ask God a question and just know His answer. Like those who hear internally, there is often a struggle of asking,"Is it just me, am I making all this up?" This is part of why the third key, deliverance from any demonic influence, is extra important. In freedom, we can hear more easily from God without having to sift through manipulation.

Often, when praying for people, I will have moments of knowing an issue they suffer from. In one instance I was praying for several people for healing but when I got to one woman whom I had never met, I "knew" she had stomach issues related to childhood trauma. I began commanding the trauma to leave her body and all effects against her stomach to be broken off. Her look of shock followed by deep weeping was a sign that what I "knew" was right on. Stepping out in faith in moments like that can increase your trust in knowing what you know!

Sensing is very similar to knowing, except there is an ever so gentle awareness that the answer is coming to you. People describe it more like a feeling or emotion but it is known in the same way as knowing. Other times, in the case of words of knowledge for healing, sensing may be a physical feeling in the body in the area where a person is having an issue. Some feel this as pain while others may feel heat, tingling, or a moving sensation in the area to be prayed for.

Visions & Images in the Mind

Visions are seen with the eyes as an open vision, or in the mind like a dream but while a person is awake. Visions can seem like your imagination, however, God gives an interpretation or a knowing of the meaning behind it and reveals more of His nature through them. Some visions are literal, while others are metaphorical. It is important to recognize what it may be or wait until God reveals the nature of it before releasing the vision publicly.

People who receive visions *see* what God is saying.

A picture or movie will play out in front of them or in their mind. These visions may be a direction for intercession, instructions for future plans, or what to do or pray at that moment. <u>Like other ways of hearing from the Father, sometimes they are simply revelations of Christ for that person meant to draw them deeper into intimacy with Him.</u>

Often I receive visions while in prayer and intercession. These help me to know the needed target for the moment as I ask God, "Father, what do you want to say today?" In those moments He will reveal key details of areas to intercede for or how He desires to move in a region. Occasionally, a demonic entity will be seen when asking this. Many fear that the enemy is trying to manipulate or interfere with their prayer time, when the reality may be that God is trying to reveal a stronghold in the area as a target.

All believers need to guard their hearts and minds. Allowing books, movies, video games, and daydreams of ungodly making will distort your ability to have a pure mind. These things added to the imagination create an overactivity of thoughts and open doors to the demonic in your life. If you want to see clearly what God is saying, put away any demonic influences that could manipulate your mind and eyes.

<u>Dreams</u>

Dreams and visions are very similar, however, dreams happen while you are asleep. Many people describe dreams in greater detail than visions. Feelings, emotions, and sensations are also more common in dreams than visions. Dreams, like visions, can be literal, metaphorical, or a combination of both.

The dream world has often been hijacked by the demonic, so discerning what is of God and what is a tactic of the enemy is important. This is another reason that deliverance is so vastly important. I will go into more specifics on nightmares in Chapter Ten.

Dreams often have an element meant for the future, whether it be the next day or years down the road. However, I have had dreams of a friend being in a very specific place I had no idea they were visiting. When I woke up, I found out that they had been at that building while I was dreaming. His Spirit was communing with mine about a current event.

One dream that massively shifted the course of my life involved a lie I believed and direction for the next steps of our lives. All my life I had dreamed of going into full-time missions. As life progressed, however, I thought that door was closed and I would have to settle for short-term trips.

One night I dreamt that I was in an airport waiting for my flight. Suddenly I realized that I had the wrong time and my flight at gate X, across the airport, was about to take off in 12 minutes. I made a mad dash across the airport to my gate. I had to go through security to get to the gate, they stopped me and looked through my bags, asking why I had so many extension cords. I ran to my gate and the attendant said they had closed the doors. However, she walked me down the ramp and began banging on the door to the plane in hopes they would let me in. The door was so heavy that they couldn't hear her banging so she finally checked to see if she could open the latch. The door wasn't even locked! She went in to ask the pilot if I could board the plane. She told the pilot, "Cherish Bickel is here and she needs to be on this flight." He became very excited when he heard my name and agreed that I needed to be on that flight! He insisted that she not tell me his name was Mark. I boarded the plane to see many Asian people wearing layers of heaviness. Mark offered me water for the long flight ahead. As passengers were chatting one mentioned that we were heading to Phnom Penh.

This dream revealed to me that the door to missions was never locked and that I was supposed to go to Phnom Penh, Cambodia. Twelve months to the day of the dream, I landed in Phnom Penh. Today, my husband, myself and four of our children now live in Cambodia. X marked the spot. I have now been through the airport in the dream many times, an airport I had never seen before that dream. I will admit that there is so much more to this dream and the revelation of it all continues to grow. There are details to it that reveal the mandate of our ministry here and the calling in my life.

God has often used dreams to reveal big changes coming in our lives, to give direction, and to bring peace in the changing seasons. In one dream He spoke to me and told me that He was moving us to a land of milk and honey and that we would strike the rock and water would flow where others had tried and failed. While looking at housing a realtor asked us, "Are you sure you can make it here? Many people move here thinking it is the land of milk and honey, but they fail." Every fear and hesitation was wiped away in that moment!

Recognition is the first step to hearing

I hope this chapter has helped you recognize the way that God may be speaking to you. This is the first step in walking through emotional healing while partnering with the Father. This is a very limited explanation for the sake of moving into healing with confidence, and there are many great resources dedicated to hearing God in specific ways, I would encourage you to grow in the way you hear best. In the next chapter, we will discuss how to be sure you are hearing God clearly, without interference from the enemy.

Activation

I will have steps in each chapter to help activate you in listening to the voice of God and using that information for healing and walking confidently as a son or daughter of the King.

1. Recognize any hindrances in allowing God to commune with you: open doors, religious mindsets, or fear. Renounce them and declare that you were made for communion (community & communication) with God.

2. Think through a time when you felt a nudging to do something and then saw the fruit of following that nudging. How did you "hear" this nudging?

3. Find a place of solitude. Clear your mind and command your thoughts to be still, ask for shalom to come over your mind. Close your eyes and ask God how He speaks to you. Listen and perceive what He is saying or showing you, or what you already seem to know. Now ask Him if there is anything He would like you to know.

Scripture References to Hearing

There are many scriptures referencing God speaking to His children, and even to people at enmity with God (EX Daniel 5:5, Genesis 41). Here are just a few references to each form of hearing.

In the last days, God says, I will pour out my Spirit on all people. Your sons and daughters will prophesy, your young men will see visions, your old men will dream dreams.
Acts 2:17 NIV

Audibly

Then I heard the voice of the Lord saying, "Whom shall I send? And who will go for us?"
And I said, "Here am I. Send me!"
Isaiah 6:8 NIV

The voice spoke to him a second time, "Do not call anything impure that God has made clean."
Acts 10:15 NIV

He fell to the ground and heard a voice say to him, "Saul, Saul, why do you persecute me?" "Who are you, Lord?" Saul asked. "I am Jesus, whom you are persecuting," he replied.
Acts 9:4-5 NIV

Internal hearing

The Spirit searches all things, even the deep things of God. For who knows a person's thoughts except their own spirit within them? In the same way no one knows the thoughts of God except the Spirit of God. What we have received is not the spirit of the world, but the Spirit who is from God, so that we may understand what God has freely given us. This is what we speak, not in words taught us by human wisdom but in words taught by the Spirit, explaining spiritual realities with Spirit-taught words. The person without the Spirit does not accept the things that come from the Spirit of God but considers them foolishness, and cannot understand them because they are discerned only through the Spirit.

1 Corinthians 2:10-14 NIV (This is an example of Internal hearing, knowing and sensing, each person will perceive the Spirit's revelation different)

Knowing/drop in the spirit

But the wisdom that comes from heaven is first of all pure; then peace-loving, considerate, submissive, full of mercy and good fruit, impartial and sincere.
James 3:17 NIV

Acts 5:1-11 Shows Peter "knowing" and having

discernment about dishonesty of others.

Sensing

We sought out the disciples there and stayed with them seven days. Through the Spirit they urged Paul not to go on to Jerusalem.
Acts 21:4 NIV (Again, internal hearing, knowing, and sensing are essentially the same, it is the perception of the person receiving the knowledge that varies.)

Visions

I, John, your brother and companion in the suffering and kingdom and patient endurance that are ours in Jesus, was on the island of Patmos because of the word of God and the testimony of Jesus. On the Lord's Day I was in the Spirit, and I heard behind me a loud voice like a trumpet, which said: "Write on a scroll what you see and send it to the seven churches: to Ephesus, Smyrna, Pergamum, Thyatira, Sardis, Philadelphia and Laodicea."

I turned around to see the voice that was speaking to me. And when I turned I saw seven golden lampstands, and among the lampstands was someone like a son of man, dressed in a robe reaching down to his feet and with a golden sash

around his chest.
Revelation 1:9-13 NIV

I will stand at my watch
    and station myself on the ramparts;
I will look to see what he will say to me,
    and what answer I am to give to this complaint.
Habakkuk 2:1 NIV

While I was still in prayer, Gabriel, the man I had seen in the earlier vision, came to me in swift flight about the time of the evening sacrifice.
Daniel 9:21 NIV

About noon the following day as they were on their journey and approaching the city, Peter went up on the roof to pray. He became hungry and wanted something to eat, and while the meal was being prepared, he fell into a trance. He saw heaven opened and something like a large sheet being let down to earth by its four corners.
Acts 10:9-16 NIV

*In Damascus there was a disciple named Ananias. The Lord **called** to him in a **vision**, "Ananias!" "Yes, Lord," he answered. The Lord **told** him, "Go to the house of Judas on Straight Street and ask for a man from Tarsus named Saul, for he is praying. In a **vision** he has seen a man named Ananias come and place his hands on him to restore his sight."*
Acts 9:10-12 NIV (bold added to show both vision and audible together)

Dreams

In the first year of Belshazzar king of Babylon, Daniel had a dream, and visions passed through his mind as he was lying in bed. He wrote down the substance of his dream.
Daniel 7:1 NIV

While Pilate was sitting on the judge's seat, his wife sent him this message: "Don't have anything to do with that innocent man, for I have suffered a great deal today in a dream because of him."
Matthew 27:19 NIV

Matthew 1 & 2 alone recount four separate dreams where direction and insight was given.

◆ ◆ ◆

2. IS THAT GOD?

Therefore, there is now no condemnation for those who are in Christ Jesus, because through Christ Jesus the law of the Spirit who gives life has set you free from the law of sin and death
Romans 8:1-2 NIV

Practice

"How do I know it's God and not me?" This question is the number one question I hear when helping others distinguish the voice of God. It is a valid concern and one we must always tread. In order to say that God spoke something we need to be certain He did! For this reason, we tell students who are learning to receive words of knowledge or prophetic words, "I feel like God is showing me..." or "I am perceiving that God may be saying..." This takes the pressure off of the person giving the word and indicates to the listener that if it doesn't sit well with them, they are welcome to let it go. It is a great idea to find someone who has shown the fruit of hearing clearly from God and sharing with them what you are perceiving. This safe space of learning and testing helps you identify if you are hearing correctly or if there may be interference.

Write out the dreams, visions, or words from the Lord that you believe you are hearing and ask a mature believer who walks in the prophetic if they can look it over. Document what you hear and watch for the fruit. Just like my dream of flying to Phnom Penh transpiring 12 months later, after seeing I had 12 "minutes" in the dream there was tangible fruit of the word God spoke to me. I am so glad I wrote it out with a date, I did not schedule the trip 12 months later; it just so happened that I landed on that day with a team. Doing this will build trust in your trust in hearing from God and will raise your confidence level as you see that God holds true to His word.

The Voice of God will NOT

God is good; He is kind and holds true to His character. He will not condemn or shame you, though He will bring conviction. Conviction is our hearts crying out for not living in alignment with God's will. It calls us to repentance and causes us to turn our lives back into alignment with God. Condemnation tells us that we will never be saved, that we are a horrible person, and that we will go to hell. This is a demonic agenda meant to keep us in a cycle of despair. This demonic condemnation is what causes those caught in cycles of addiction to go to drugs and alcohol over and over. It is a voice that says, "You are a loser, a monster who can never be saved. No one, not even God could love a person like you. Why bother?" Shame does the same, equally demonic, and often sounds like, "You are filthy, you aren't good for anything. Look at what you have done and who you have hurt. No one would love you if they knew the real you. God knows."

Conviction, however, comes from love. Conviction says, "This is not who you were meant to be. You have a greater purpose and destiny. Leave these things behind and see what lies ahead for you." Conviction creates true repentance and allowing us to turn to the image we were created in, while shame and condemnation can cause people to put away sins of the flesh for a time- it never changes the heart. Hearts are changed when love is allowed in, not through fear.

The voice of God will not lead you to bitterness, to hate others, or to judge others. God does reveal behaviors or actions to those who are in a place of authority to do something about it, but He does not place judgment, hate, or bitterness on the word of knowledge. Mature leaders will choose to love and walk with a person out of the issue, should the individual so choose.

When discerning God's voice, He will not say negative things about you. His voice is always loving, gentle, and guiding, though at times there can be urgency. His voice uplifts, edifies, encourages, gives direction, comfort, healing, and guidance. His voice will always align with His Word.

This should go without saying, but His voice will never tell you to sin or harm others. Unfortunately, there are many caught up in sinful acts that claim God told them to do it.

Renunciations

I want to offer some renunciation to break off any demonic holds that may keep you from hearing God's voice to the fullest. Repeat these out loud with authority. Pay attention to any shifts in thoughts, feelings, and emotions as you say these. These are declarations you are making canceling any agreements. You are not speaking to God in doing this, you are declaring it to the authorities, against the powers of this dark world and against the spiritual forces of evil in the heavenly realms. With that, take authority! Speak boldly!

In the name of Jesus, I take authority back over my mind, my dreams, my hearing, and my vision. I renounce any areas where I have denied the authority and ability of God to

speak to me. I renounce denial of the Holy Spirit and His desire to commune with those He loves. I renounce all fear that has kept me from trusting in the voice of God.

Going back to Adam and Eve, In the name of Jesus, I renounce every curse against me and my bloodline, especially any curses that are meant to hinder my relationship and fellowship with God. I declare I was meant to walk in the cool of the day with the Father, talking to Him and listening to Him. I declare He desires to commune with me daily.

In the name of Jesus, I renounce the lie that I am not good enough to hear from God and every word curse I have spoken over myself or that has been spoken over me saying that I cannot hear God. I renounce the false doctrines that tell me that God no longer moves in the lives of believers.

Many doors can be opened by what we watch and allow in our lives through games, media, etc. We want to close these doors and cut off all manipulation of our imagination.

In the name of Jesus, I renounce watching movies, shows, & clips that allow demonic influence to my mind, my eyes, my ears, and my dreams. I renounce playing evil video games and fantasy role-playing games and the effect they have had on my mind. I renounce reading inappropriate books, magazines, and blogs and all the effects they have had on my dreams and imagination. I renounce all fantasizing and ungodly daydreaming that has allowed the enemy to play freely in my mind.

By the authority of Christ in me, I cancel out all curses allowed in by these actions. I break them off of me and my bloodline right now. I command any demon that gained access through these things to leave me now in the name of Jesus Christ. Go to the pit now!

Father, I give you permission to speak to me. Forgive me for any time I have denied Your power and desire to know me and be known by me. I give You the freedom to speak to me however You desire. Help me to discern Your voice clearly and move in accordance with Your word. Thank you for loving me and pursuing me!

Father, I bless my children and future bloodline to know You and to commune with You, to hear Your voice, and to trust in You. I bless their purity and pursuit of knowing You more.

Father, sanctify my mind and imagination. Make it pure and holy before You. I ask that You remove any trauma, thoughts, or memories that cause unholy images to come into my thoughts or dreams. Search me and find if there is any grievous way in me. I ask You to root it out of my life.

In the beautiful name of Jesus, I pray, Amen.

Activation

1. Take a moment to daydream with God. Think of a big God adventure that has been on your heart and ask Him to shape and mold it. Ask Him what He has to say about it. Journal what He shows you.

2. Each morning when you wake up, say good morning to the Father, Jesus, and Holy Spirit. Ask them what they want you to know that day. Jot it down, even on a note on your phone. At the end of the day, see how that applied. This is a great daily practice for learning to hear His voice.

◆ ◆ ◆

3. RECOGNIZE & UPROOT

Do not conform to the pattern of this world, but be transformed by the renewing of your mind. Then you will be able to test and approve what God's will is—his good, pleasing, and perfect will.
Romans 12:2 NIV

My first emotional healing took place lying in bed one evening. I was in emotional turmoil months after a betrayal that gripped my heart. I couldn't get through a single day without intense pain and sadness, my heart felt ripped in half-physically. My husband told me to ask God about it. God kindly revealed to me that I had not forgiven as I thought I had. He showed me the bitterness that had manifested as pain. I forgave the person, and in that moment I was instantly healed of the pain that had plagued me for six months. He then revealed to me that if I held on to unforgiveness it would hold me back from the nations! I cannot imagine where I would be now if I had not let Him heal me.

Strongholds

Now that we have covered hearing the voice of God, it is time to dive into greater levels of freedom! The next step to freedom is recognizing strongholds. Strongholds are thought processes that have been repeated and believed so many times that a fortress in the mind is created, a way of thinking that repeats over and over in a pattern that tears down the person. Demonic strongholds can bind us up with fear, anxiety, depression, worthlessness, shame, pain, rejection, self-hatred, abandonment, insecurity, bitterness, hatred, and victimhood, among other painful mentalities.

When a traumatic event or painful moment happens and we believe one of these thoughts, it then places a root or foundation of trauma that can easily be built upon. We hear a confirming thought, believe it and another brick is added until a house is built for a demon to live in, a stronghold that becomes a natural pattern of thinking. It hides the demonic behind self-degradation. We walk through deliverance to kick the demon out and often much of the house gets broken down at that moment. However, there is a process of renewing the mind that must be walked out on the part of the believer.

This process breaks down any remnants of the stronghold and teaches the mind right thinking in its place.

New Patterns

I am adamant that all believers who go through deliverance should be given "homework" to destroy the strongholds and build up a new way of thinking. Science backs up this spiritual truth showing neuroplasticity that can be reshaped through habits. If you continually renew your mind by replacing the lies of the enemy with God's truth, your mind will begin to create new neural pathways that form patterns of right thinking that are in line with who God says you are. After identifying the root of the pain and addressing that, we then begin to break down the way of thinking that was formed through the trauma. We will cover these steps later in the chapter, and then repeat them for each mindset or pain.

Trauma

Trauma is often a gateway that allows evil into our lives. While this may not be fair, it is an access point of the enemy and creates the foundation for unhealthy thought patterns. I have never met a person who has not been through some form of trauma. Many people, however, brush it off as if it is not a big deal to avoid facing the problem. This coping mechanism often buries the issue but allows it to manifest in other ways. Unforgiveness may manifest as anger instead of bitterness, with the anger rarely being directed to the offender, but rather, directed at others close to the person.

Our brain perceives several things as trauma, including; car accidents to bullying, rape, or witnessing violence, diagnoses, and so much more. Self-protective measures begin to take place to numb the pain and lies begin to take root. The easiest way to identify possible traumas in one's life is to break down life stages and pinpoint any trauma, embarrassment, or emotional events that took place.

On the following page, take a moment to write down instances that happened at various ages. This is simply to help you think through time periods. Remember to write down any events that could have been perceived by your brain as traumatic, even if you see it as being okay.

0-5 years old

_____

_____

6-10 years old

_____

_____

11-15 years old

_____

_____

16+ years old

_____

_____

_____

(Brewer, 2022)

Now that you have identified possible points of trauma, repeat the following for each:

In the name of Jesus Christ, I renounce the trauma of _____ I renounce every curse of trauma and break it off of me and my bloodline. I command all trauma to leave my body. Everywhere where trauma has been stored in my body, I command it to release and leave now. Body, I command you to be healed and free of pain and infirmity.

Father, I thank You that I can be free of the pain and torment of trauma by Your miracle-working power. I ask that You bind my heart as one, healing all fractures and wounds and making me whole. I thank You that You bind up the brokenhearted and bring complete restoration. I ask that You bring healing to all parts of my body and soul. In Jesus

name, Amen.

<u>Forgiveness</u>

If the trauma was caused by another person, repeat the following:

Father, by Your grace, I choose to forgive _____ (person who hurt you) for _____ (what they did) even though it made me feel _____ (emotions). I release this person from all bitterness and judgment and instead I choose to bless them with _____.

This prayer was adapted from Mike Brewer's Self-Deliverance Guide: A Step-by-step Guide to Freedom from Bondage and Closing of Spiritual Doors. This book is a fantastic resource for people desiring freedom and learning to walk in deliverance.

This is a good time to pause, practice hearing from God, and ask Holy Spirit if there is anyone else you need to forgive today. After listening, go ahead and walk through the declaration of forgiveness for those He reveals as well.

<u>Soul Ties</u>

Soul Ties are created in healthy and unhealthy relationships. For instance, David and Jonathan had a deep friendship that resulted in their souls being "knit together." When a couple is married they become one, and when a person submits to a spiritual authority or any other commitment or covenant they often form a tie. These soul ties are healthy so long as the relationship is healthy.

Unhealthy soul ties are created in cases of abuse, manipulation, partnering with another in the occult, sex outside of marriage, control, and blood pacts (including some tattoos). Each of these ties should be broken and cut off. Often, people with these types of ties will have frequent dreams of the other person or feel controlled by their opinions even when far apart. Thankfully, breaking these ties is an easy process in which many people have found immediate release and freedom.

After renouncing the trauma caused by the person and forgiving them say:

In the name of Jesus Christ, I renounce all unholy activities I partnered with with _____(name). I sever and break every spiritual, sexual, or covenant tie with _____(name). I cut this tie now by the power and the blood of Jesus.

If you are still in a relationship with the person, such as a previously abusive spouse, instead say:

In the name of Jesus Christ, I cut off every unholy tie and bond between _____ and myself leaving only what is holy and pure. I place the blood of Jesus between _____ and myself.

Identifying the Root of Emotions

Now that you know how to begin to recognize
strongholds (we will go into more detail on specific
emotions in the next chapters), have identified
trauma, have forgiven those who have hurt you, and
have broken soul ties, we can address the root of
strongholds much more easily.

Choose one stronghold at a time to work on. You
will need to focus on one mindset or emotion at a
time to find healing. Find a quiet place where you
can hear from the Lord and allow for time to rest in
His presence, listen to Him, and respond. Be aware
that this process may uncover some pretty deep
emotions. Some people find it helpful to journal
the questions that they are asking God and His
response.
First, pray:

**Father, I desire to be free of all negative self-talk
and emotions. I ask that You search me and find
any grievous way in me and uproot it so I can be
free and walk boldly in my identity. Help me to
hear Your voice and overcome all lies of the enemy
today. I invite you to come and show me the root
of this pain. Holy Spirit, come bring Your comfort
and shine Your light on the painful areas You want
to heal.**

Now that you have invited the presence of God,

walk through these steps for each stronghold or mentality one at a time. Complete the steps for each wound before stopping. Press in even when the emotions are painful. Find a quiet place where you can be alone with God without distractions. Still your mind and focus on the presence of God.

Step 1: Identify the emotion; what is one specific stronghold you want to work on today?

Step 2: Identify the beginning of this affliction by asking, "Holy Spirit, where did this lie first get in?"

Step 3: When a memory of pain is revealed, renounce the trauma of the moment, break any soul ties with offenders, and ask God, "What lie did I begin believing in this moment?"

Step 4: Renounce the lies you have believed, repent for believing a false identity, and ask God, "Father, what is the truth?" Write down the truth He reveals to you.
Additionally, you can ask:
"What do You want me to know about that moment?"
"Where were You at that moment?"
"Is there anything else You would like me to know?"

Step 5: Receive the truth and declare the following: "I declare that _____ (God's truth). I cut all ties with the enemy and tear down the strongholds the enemy has placed in my mind of _____ and I choose to believe His truth about my identity as a son/daughter of the Most High King.

Use these tools over and over as often as needed for your full healing. Once you have identified the root of a stronghold and walked through these steps, there is still a process of renewing the mind that must be walked out. While much of the pain goes simply by receiving truth, we must continue to be transformed by the renewing of our minds. An example of this process can be found in the final note.

Mind Renewal

The process of mind renewal is quite simple and done daily until our brains form new pathways of thinking, and then we still do it when the enemy tries to attack. These simple steps will become easier each day that you put them into practice until they become a natural way of life.

Step 1: Recognize a negative thought. Catch it the moment it begins and declare (out loud if possible) that it is a lie and does not belong in your mind.

Step 2: Replace that lie with spiritual truth. Scripture is the best weapon, but any Biblical truth, even if not verbatim, is a weapon. Remember the truths that God spoke to you when identifying the root and use that truth often.

Each of the following chapters contains scriptures and identity statements that can be wielded against lies quickly. Write them down or memorize them so they are always accessible.

Mind Renewal Example

The thought "I'm worthless" comes to mind. You say (preferably out loud), "That is a lie, I was bought with a high price (1 Corinthians 6:20), and I am exceedingly valuable (Matthew 6:26)." Or simply, "I recognize that is a lie, the truth is that the Word of God says I am exceedingly valuable and that Christ died for me!"

Be prepared with scriptures and spiritual truths that oppose the lies you may commonly face. Commit them to memory so you have a quick weapon to pull out. We will cover specific mindsets and emotions in the following chapters and the truth spoken in the Word which will help you to speak true identity over yourself.

Activation

1. Pay close attention to your thoughts and self-talk for 24 hours. Are

there any negative thoughts about yourself? What thoughts were the most common?

2. Look in a mirror and record every thought that comes to mind. Are there any thoughts you need to work through the pattern of mind renewal? Start by renouncing the word curses you spoke over your body, then begin blessing the parts of your body that you spoke down about.

◆ ◆ ◆

4. BREAKING REJECTION

For the Lord will not reject his people;
*   he will never forsake his inheritance.*
Psalm 94:14 NIV

I don't know that I have sat with many people who have not at one point or another struggled with rejection. I imagine if I walked into a middle or high school and asked, "Who here has felt rejected?" every hand would shoot high. We have all experienced it. The issue isn't *if* someone was rejected, it is if they felt rejected and allowed the thoughts to simmer and shape them. Rejection happens every day but how we perceive it can be from a healthy mindset, whereby not taking it personally, or it can be from a wound of rejection, which can cause a negative thought processes to cascade.

Allow me to share an example:

Two women are standing at the grocery store checkout lines. A bagger looks at them both but then goes on to the next conveyor. One woman has no stronghold of rejection and assumes the bagger saw a bigger need in the next aisle, so she forgets about it immediately and goes about her day. The other woman has a stronghold of rejection and assumes the bagger doesn't like something about her. These thoughts may partner with self-condemnation and thoughts of self-hatred. Another brick of rejection is added to the stronghold. She then begins to replay the scene and wonder what he didn't like about her, and thoughts of worthlessness and self-degradation begin to ruminate. In reality, the bagger saw two able-bodied women and, on the other side of them, a mother struggling to hold her baby, keep her toddler seated, and bag her groceries simultaneously.

It sounds silly when we read it, but this is a very common thought process that many people struggle with. The enemy wants nothing more than for the children of God to believe they are not loved and wanted. Thoughts of rejection when they become a pattern become stronger and more easily triggered by the most innocent of behaviors.

This rejection and insecurity play out dangerously in our relationships. They are often causing arguments and assumptions that are really just built-up accusations in the mind. Rejection frequently comes with thoughts that say something along the lines of, "No one loves you, you aren't wanted, others will be chosen before you, others are liked more than you, you won't be invited, or you intentionally were not invited in because someone didn't want you around." There are many variations to these thoughts and it is not an all-inclusive list, but rather, a starting point to identify if this is an area that you need to work on. All of these are thoughts that may or may not be based on reality. Often, when thoughts of rejection occur, the thoughts become stronger until a pattern is formed that then affects our outward behavior which can then cause others to reject, or not want to be around the self-pitying state of assumed rejection.

While curses are associated with rejection, causing others to reject a person, most rejection stems from an initial trauma and the following brick-by-brick thoughts received. As mentioned, this can push others to begin to reject as the thoughts become the personality. Whether perceived or true rejection, it is worth declaring the following:

In the name of Jesus Christ, I renounce rejection and the demon of rejection. I renounce all thoughts and words of rejection and all word curses of rejection that I have spoken over myself. I renounce the accusations against others formed in my mind. I break the curse of rejection off of me and my bloodline now and command every demon to go to the pit now!

Self-Imposed Rejection

Self-imposed rejection varies from rejection only in that it is a self-sabotaging thought process that leads pushing others away. The thought is that others will reject you first, so you will give them a reason to reject OR that others will reject you, so you will just back off to avoid the pain. This thought can cause you to begin pushing others away and isolating yourself for fear of the pain of rejection that was never implied by others. In reality, it allows more pain of rejection and a lifestyle of rejection to set in.

Self-imposed rejection is one of the most somber situations to watch. As you reach out to show love to others, they push away only to accuse you of rejecting them. It becomes a cycle of rejection as the one who assumes they are rejected responds to love by rejecting others.

Perceived Rejection

Perceived rejection occurs when the pattern of rejection grows to assume others are rejecting you even when they are not. Like the scenario in the grocery store, this is a built-up stronghold that creates a behavior of rejection.

In the case of perceived rejection, assumptions and

accusations are made about others. If this is the case, conversations of repentance may need to take place as you are freed of rejection. This is especially important in marriage when one spouse perceives rejection from the other. Open communication must happen so healing can take place in the relationship. It is guaranteed that if one spouse has falsely perceived rejection, it will play out at some point in reactions and communication. Acknowledge that you wrongly sensed rejection and you would like your spouse to co-labor with you to break the hold of rejection by helping you recognize the behaviors.

In the name of Jesus Christ, I renounce self-imposed and perceived rejection. I renounce self-sabotage, rejecting others, false self-protection, and the demon of rejection. I renounce the assumptions, accusations, and bitterness towards others. I further renounce all thoughts and accusations that I have been rejected by God. I renounce and cut off all generational curses related to perceived rejection, bitterness, and self-sabotage from me and my bloodline, now.

If you have identified rejection in your life, follow the steps to identifying the root trauma or pain in Chapter Three, then the process of mind renewal, also in Chapter Three. Memorize the identity statements and scriptures in this chapter to have as weapons on hand when thoughts of rejection come your way. Remember to recognize these thoughts and cut them down quickly and continuously until they are no longer a stronghold in your life.

Identity Statements

I am not rejected, I am loved, wanted, and chosen.
I was chosen before the foundations of the world by the Creator who destined me for His purposes.
I am accepted and loved in the family of God.
God's grace is sufficient for me.
God calls me His own.
I will not be condemned, instead, I live free in Christ.

Scripture

I will not forget you!
See, I have engraved you on the palms of my hands;
    your walls are ever before me.
Isaiah 49:15b-16 NIV

For the Lord will not reject his people;
    he will never forsake his inheritance.
Psalm 94:14 NIV

"A new command I give you: Love one another. As I have loved you, so you must love one another. By this everyone will know that you are my disciples; if you love one another."
John 13:34-35 NIV

Therefore, there is now no condemnation for those who are in Christ Jesus, because through Christ Jesus the law of the Spirit who gives life has set you free from the law of sin and death.
Romans 8:1-2 NIV

What, then, shall we say in response to these things? If God is for us, who can be against us? He who did not spare his own Son, but gave him up for us all—how will he not also, along with him, graciously give us all things? Who will bring any charge against those whom God has chosen? It is God who justifies. Who then is the one who condemns? No one. Christ Jesus who died —more than that, who was raised to life—is at the right hand of God and is also interceding for us. Who shall separate us from the love of Christ? Shall trouble or hardship or persecution or famine or nakedness or danger or sword?
Romans 8:31-35

Mind Renewal Example

The thought of, "No one will like you, they will reject you," comes at you. You swing back with, "That is a lie of the enemy, I am loved, wanted, and accepted in the family of God."

OR

Thoughts of rejection & insecurity attack. Declare, "I

will not partner with the lies of the enemy, I declare the Lord will not reject his people; He will never forsake his inheritance." (Psalm 94:14)

Activation

1. Repeat the identity statements out loud each morning for three weeks and follow the mind renewal steps. Journal how your thoughts change over the course of three weeks.

2. Pray for the people you have felt rejected by who are still in your life. After praying say, "In the name of Jesus, I choose to bless _____ (name) with _____." Pay attention to how your thoughts towards them change in the coming weeks.

◆ ◆ ◆

5. LEAVING ABANDONMENT BEHIND

For those who are led by the Spirit of God are the children of God. 15 The Spirit you received does not make you slaves, so that you live in fear again; rather, the Spirit you received brought about your adoption to sonship. And by Him, we cry, "Abba, Father." The Spirit himself testifies with our spirit that we are God's children. Now if we are children, then we are heirs— heirs of God and co-heirs with Christ, if indeed we share in his sufferings in order that we may also share in his glory.
Romans 8:14-17 NIV

Abandonment

Abandonment can be rooted in truly painful experiences or in perception. Many children go through awful circumstances that can create trauma and the fear of abandonment. Others, being at a young age, perceive abandonment from an innocent circumstance such as their being left at a babysitter's house whom they did not know or their parent leaving for an extended work trip. In their young imagination, it may have seemed like a longer time, or the fear in the moment allowed abandonment to take root.

Abandonment often will play out in almost indistinguishable thoughts. I had no clue that I struggled with abandonment until one circumstance tipped the scales for the thoughts to become even louder.

Suddenly, I began hearing loudly, "Everyone else in your life has left you at some point, everyone else will too." I began to realize that the underlying thought had been whispering for a long time. Within two weeks of these thoughts becoming louder, God, in His grace, appeared before me, took my hand, and spoke directly to my heart promising that He would never leave me or abandon me. He repeated the same phrase over and over, and He never said a word about anyone else. Yet, His voice broke through the thoughts and destroyed the stronghold in an instant. I was so strongly set free at that moment that I was immediately released from it and able to tell my husband the thoughts I had been fighting. I was filled with joy and peace, all doubt and fear gone! This is why I strongly believe in the necessity of Believers to hear from God for themselves.

Abandonment can play out as jealousy, people pleasing, a fear of change, or needing constant reassurance that one is loved. Abandonment and rejection may or may not be rooted in the same traumatic event. It is important to recognize curses and trauma in order to break any cycles so they do not pass on to the next generation.

People pleasing and a fear of doing something to push away loved ones are very common along with the fear of a spouse leaving or cheating. Often those who struggle with abandonment will habitually apologize and, if they think they did or said something offensive, they will ask for reassurance, even if there was no indication the other person was offended. There may be a fear of not being loved or a fear of loving others because love brings pain. Some people may have struggled with doubts that God could love them unconditionally.

Declare the following statements out loud to break any bondages of abandonment:

In the name of Jesus Christ, I renounce abandonment and perceived abandonment. I renounce the demons of fear and abandonment. I renounce the assumptions, accusations, and fear of others leaving. I further renounce all thoughts and accusations of the enemy that I will be abandoned by God. I renounce and cut

off all generational curses related to perceived abandonment from me and my bloodline, now.

If any of this resonates with you, follow the steps of finding the root in Chapter Three, then the steps of mind renewal, also in Chapter Three. Memorize the following statements and scriptures to be ready to hold up the shield of faith against the enemy's fiery arrows. Remember, renewal of the mind is not a one-time task, but an ongoing process to retrain your brain to righteous thinking.

Identity Statements

I am a child of God, He cares for me.
I have been adopted into the family of God.
God loves me with everlasting love.
God will never leave me nor forsake me.
I have the mind of Christ.
Perfect love has cast out fear and the bonds of fear are broken.
I am created to live in covenant relationships.
My heart is secure, God guards my heart.

Scripture

For those who are led by the Spirit of God are the children of God. The Spirit you received does not make you slaves so that you live in fear again; rather,

the Spirit you received brought about your adoption to sonship. And by Him, we cry, "Abba, Father." The Spirit himself testifies with our spirit that we are God's children. 17 Now if we are children, then we are heirs—heirs of God and co-heirs with Christ, if indeed we share in his sufferings in order that we may also share in his glory.
Romans 8:14-17 NIV

The righteous cry out, and the Lord hears them;
*   he delivers them from all their troubles.*
The Lord is close to the brokenhearted
*   and saves those who are crushed in spirit.*

The righteous person may have many troubles,
*   but the Lord delivers him from them all;*
he protects all his bones,
*   not one of them will be broken.*
Psalm 34:17-20 NIV

The LORD himself goes before you and will be with you; he will never leave you nor forsake you. Do not be afraid; do not be discouraged."
Deuteronomy 31:8 NIV

God sets the lonely in families,
*   he leads out the prisoners with singing;*
*   but the rebellious live in a sun-scorched land.*
Psalm 68:6 NIV

I am with you always, to the very end of the age.
Matthew 28:20b NIV

Do not let your hearts be troubled. You believe in

God[a]; believe also in me. My Father's house has many rooms; if that were not so, would I have told you that I am going there to prepare a place for you? And if I go and prepare a place for you, I will come back and take you to be with me that you also may be where I am. You know the way to the place where I am going."
John 14:1-4 NIV

Mind Renewal Example

The thought, "You will be left alone forever" hits. You hit back with, "Abandonment is a lie of the enemy, I am a child of God and His perfect love has cast out fear."

OR

Thoughts of abandonment come along. Respond with, "Abandonment is a lie, Christ declares that He will be with me forever." (*Matthew 28:20*)

Activation

1. If you recognize abandonment in your life, take time with God and allow Him to show you where the root took place. Use the tools in Chapter Three under Identifying the Root of Emotions. Allow God to bring healing to that moment.

2. Create a simple, easy-to-memorize rebuttal for when these thoughts come on. Put it on a sticky note in your car so you see it daily.

◆ ◆ ◆

6. DESTROYING THE LIES OF WORTHLESSNESS & SELF-HATRED

How precious are your thoughts about me, O God. They cannot be numbered! I can't even count them; they outnumber the grains of sand! And when I wake up, you are still with me!
Psalms 139:17-18 NLT

<u>Learning Self-worth</u>

Worthlessness seeks to beat down an individual from the inside out. Often, the lie that 'you aren't good enough' begins at an early age or after repeated feelings of failure during the formative years. It is often spoken over individuals by parents and grandparents who are facing their own spiritual battles, and is often a repeated cycle continuing? from one generation to the next until someone breaks the cycle.

The thoughts that say, "I am no good, I am just a failure, I always screw things up, I will never succeed, and nobody could ever love me," grow until they no longer stay in the head. They begin to come out of one's mouth as they speak word curses over themselves, and eventually over their own children. Thank God, we can break these habits and learn new ones that will launch us into success and joy!

Psychology will tell you that if you believe you cannot do something, that belief will prove true. Similarly, if you believe you can do something, that belief will prove true. Changing thoughts like, 'I can't do this, I am not good at anything' to 'I can do all things through Christ who strengthens me' can change the outcome of what you are facing. At the very least, it will change your attitude and give you the strength to try again, and your children will watch you, learn your perseverance, and emulate it.

It is recorded that Thomas Edison failed 2,774 times before making a successful lightbulb. Edison once said, "I have not failed 10,000 times—I've successfully found 10,000 ways that will not work." What makes him well-known is his successes and the fact he would not give up. He had an attitude that, even in failure, there was something to be gained. This is the mindset of the most successful people- that every mistake is an opportunity for learning and growing.

Failures and mistakes will happen, but how we deal with them and what we think about ourselves in those moments can change the final outcome in our lives and future generations. Begin to recognize these thoughts and cut them off at the root. Start by breaking the curses and follow up with continual mind renewal until you have a new outlook on how precious and loved you are.

In the name of Jesus Christ, I renounce every lie that says I am a failure, I am worthless, I cannot do anything right, I am a screw-up, I am unlovable, and I will never succeed. I renounce all lies that come against my self-worth and every word curse spoken by myself or others. I break them off of me and my bloodline now.

Now pray:

Father, I thank you that you have given me the mind of Christ and that I can do all things through Christ who strengthens me. I thank you that I am loved, valued, and desired. I thank you that I am precious to you and that you desire me and have good plans for me. Will you show me Your approval and make my efforts successful? In the name of Jesus, Amen

Self Hatred

Self-hatred is another attack on the person's mind and body that will directly affect their relationships. We are instructed to love others as ourselves, which first requires that we love ourselves! For many, this is easier said than done. When worthlessness turns to self-hatred, thoughts and words of self-destruction ruin their sense of worth, value, and belonging.

To add insult to injury, parts of the church have claimed that self-hatred is holy humility. The truth is, you cannot hate yourself and agree that we are made in God's image. This dichotomy needs to be addressed in order to move forward in your freedom. Do you believe the Bible to be true? If yes, then you agree that you were made in the image of God and are being transformed into the likeness of Christ.

There are many different lies and word curses associated with self-hatred. Often, these thoughts and spoken agreements are directed at specific attributes and parts of the body. Some examples include:"I hate the way I laugh," "I hate how awkward I am," "I can't stand my voice," and "I hate my body/stomach/face/hair." Once these thoughts build up a stronghold they begin to come out as whispers as we look in a mirror and later as 'jokes' as we belittle ourselves through humor.

For years I would look in the mirror and speak word curses over my body. I would often state how much I hated my stomach. It comes as no surprise that I began having daily stomach issues for years. Once I learned to love my body and bless it as a temple of the Holy Spirit, the daily IBS symptoms went away. I would love to say that I am free of all stomach issues now, but some remain, though, they are all manageable with careful eating. The daily pain, however, is gone along with the other symptoms that came with it.

Like worthlessness, when parents deal with self-hatred it is important to catch these thoughts of self-degradation immediately and use the steps of mind renewal to replace them with the truth before they begin to come out in front of our children, or worse, directed at children. We have all heard parents belittle their children about the things they are most insecure about. For example, a parent self-conscious about their weight may speak down about their child's weight.

If these are thoughts you have experienced, follow the steps in Chapter Three to find healing at the root of the pain, then begin using the mind renewal steps also in Chapter Three for ongoing freedom. Use the following declarations to break any spiritual bondages linked to self-hatred.

In the name of Jesus Christ, I break all word curses I have spoken over myself or that others spoke over me. I break any word curses I have spoken over my children. I break the curses of hatred over my behaviors and body. I break off every infirmity that

was allowed in through these curses and I break the binding confusion over my mind. I renounce the demons behind these thoughts and lies and I command them to leave me now.

Now pray:

Father, I thank you for my body. I thank you that I am made beautifully in your image. I thank You that Your spirit dwells in me and that my body is a temple of the Living God. I repent for speaking negatively about your creation and how You made me. In Jesus' name, amen.

In Jesus' name, I bless my body to be healthy and well. I bless my body to look and function as it was intended. I bless my _____ (area you have previously spoken negatively about) and declare that it was made in the image of Christ. I call forth shalom of the Kingdom over my _____ and mind.

Use the following identity statements and scriptures to speak truth over yourself whenever these thoughts come your way.

Identity Statements

I am valuable; God sent His Son for **me**!
I am beautifully made; I was made in the image of Christ.
I am intelligent; I have the mind of Christ.
Nothing is too hard for me; I can do all things

through Christ.
I am willing and able to do hard things.
I am loved and I love myself.
I am worthy of love.
My body is amazing, it is the temple of the living God.
Resurrection power lives in me!

<u>Scripture</u>

For God so loved the world that he gave his one and only Son, that whoever believes in him shall not perish but have eternal life.
John 3:16 NIV

For you created my inmost being; you knit me together in my mother's womb. I praise you because I am fearfully and wonderfully made; your works are wonderful, I know that full well.
Psalm 139:13-14 NIV

I can do all this through him who gives me strength.
Philippians 4:13 NIV

Love the Lord your God with all your heart and with all your soul and with all your mind and with all your strength.'[a] 31 The second is this: 'Love your neighbor as yourself.'[b] There is no commandment greater than these."
Mark 12:30-31 NIV

So God created mankind in his own image,
    in the image of God he created them;
    male and female he created them.

Genesis 1:27 NIV

You were bought at a price. Therefore honor God with your bodies.
1 Corinthians 6:20 NIV

And we all, who with unveiled faces contemplate the Lord's glory, are being transformed into his image with ever-increasing glory, which comes from the Lord, who is the Spirit.
2 Corinthians 3:18

What you heard from me, keep as the pattern of sound teaching, with faith and love in Christ Jesus. 14 Guard the good deposit that was entrusted to you—guard it with the help of the Holy Spirit who lives in us.
2 Timothy 1:13-14 NIV

Mind Renewal Example

When you hear the thought, "You are so ugly," declare, "That is a lie, I am made beautifully in the image of Christ. He knit me together exactly as He intended."

OR

When thoughts of worthlessness come on, respond with, "I do not partner with worthlessness, I declare I was bought with a high price." (1 Corinthians 6:20)

Activation

1. If you recognize worthlessness or self-hatred in your life, take time with God and allow Him to show you where the root took place. Use the tools in Chapter Three under Identifying the Root of Emotions. Allow God to bring healing to that moment.

2. Create a simple, easy-to-memorize rebuttal for when these thoughts come on. Put a sticky note on your mirror with these counterattacks so you see it daily.

3. Close your eyes and ask God, how do You see me? Write down what you see and share with a mentor.

◆ ◆ ◆

7. BITTERNESS, VICTIMHOOD, AND POVERTY

Let all bitterness and wrath and anger and clamor and slander be put away from you, along with all malice. Be kind to one another, tenderhearted, forgiving one another, as God in Christ forgave you.
Ephesians 4:31-32

Mindsets Against Others

This may seem like an odd grouping, but all three of these mindsets focus on self above others. These thoughts all put the individual as the victim and the one who is owed something. They all can create habits of greed, pride, and self-righteousness.

Bitterness

Bitterness grows from unforgiveness toward others and becomes a way of life. The thoughts of what was done play over and over, and the pain and the anger are given free space in the mind and can even begin to cause health issues. As the bitterness grows, it affects all conversations because everything is seen through the lens of affliction.

We have all met people who allowed their lives to be known for the bitterness they hold. In the South, we refer to them as spittin' venom.' These people can walk into a room and shift the atmosphere to negativity. Many of these people grow up in a place of brokenness, then, through recycled patterns, may get hurt as an adult and decide that they won't let it happen again. A vow of bitterness is made. It may sound like, "I will never let anyone hurt me like that again," and so, they allow bitterness to grow like a briar patch around their hearts.

Common bitter thoughts people experience can include, "They hurt me, they need to pay," If I forgive them, I am letting them off the hook. I want to forgive them, but I want them to be punished for what they did. I am so hurt, I don't know if I will ever be okay." The desire for "justice" underlines each of the thoughts. The reality, however, is that Christ declared that we must forgive others to be forgiven ourselves. Ouch. That can be a tough pill to swallow, but with the measure you give, it will be poured out to you. I would prefer a great measure of mercy over judgment!

When we walk through forgiveness, we hand the person over to Christ, the judge, knowing that He will offer them the same mercy He offers us. We choose to forgive and release the person from all debt to us. This does not negate the need for legal action in the case of crimes, or imply that you should not report abuses. We can have a right standing in the world and forgive freely.

Bitterness puts the accuser in more bondage than the accused. Forgiveness, by Rodney Hogue, is a great resource for deep wounds, however, the tools in Chapter Three, Forgiveness & Soul Ties, may be used now to work through forgiveness layer by layer. Do not be surprised if you find freedom from hurt one day, then a few weeks later recognize another wound the person left behind. Walk through the steps again until you have fully forgiven the offensive of each person.

Break all ties with bitterness by declaring:

In the name of Jesus Christ, I break free from the bondage of bitterness, hate, and unforgiveness. I renounce these thoughts and all word curses I spoke from bitterness. I renounce the demons behind these behaviors and break them off of me and my bloodline. I command all demons to leave me now!

Father, by Your grace, I choose to forgive those who have hurt me. Help me to recognize when I am

trying to take your place as judge. I bless those who have hurt and offended me and release them from all judgments now. In Jesus' name, Amen.

Victim Mindset

The victim mindset is most commonly built up by a lifestyle of bitterness. Once the stronghold of bitterness is built, everything and everyone seems to be offensive and hurtful. This mindset causes one to see oneself as the victim of every circumstance, even when they are not involved! Those with a victim mentality often jump from church to church getting "hurt" by circumstances that didn't involve them or very minor offenses, and sometimes it is because they felt the leadership team didn't believe their stories of victimhood.

When the victim mindset grows it can become extremely destructive and form demonic false narratives. These false narratives further destroy relationships and lives. It is best to forgive others as soon as an offense happens before it becomes destructive to your life! Remember, unforgiveness begets bitterness, bitterness begets victimhood, and victimhood begets false narratives akin to borderline personality disorder.

If any of this resonates with you, begin to root it out of your life and bloodline immediately! Follow the example set in Chapter 3 of finding the root, forgiveness, breaking soul ties, and mind renewal, and also declare:

In the name of Jesus Christ, I renounce the spirits of bitterness, pain, and victimhood. I renounce giving in to false narratives and imaginations of others mistreating me. I renounce the lie that I am powerless and will always be the victim. I renounce the destruction caused by this way of thinking and putting myself before others. I renounce not helping others when they need it. I renounce breaking relationships out of offense. I break these curses off of me and my bloodline and command every demon to leave now!

Poverty Mindset

The poverty mindset is very similar to the victim mindset, except instead of being focused on offense, it is focused on not having enough. However, it can be partnered with victimhood. This can relate to money, food, things, or even the love of God. The thoughts can be, "If they succeed I can't," or, "There won't be enough." I have watched this play out as people learn to pray for healing. Those with a poverty mindset think that if someone else sees miracles happen, God's miracle power will run out and they won't see one. This is another lie that when spoken out, seems absurd, but the enemy loves to trap people in the lies they are afraid to share, layering lies with shame. But again, these thoughts are focused on the individual's well-being above those around them.

I frequently tell people that one of the keys to happiness is not looking at yourself, but rather, looking to serving others, putting others above yourself. You cannot be miserable when your focus is on God and serving others. The poverty mindset can both keep someone from serving with the thought they need to be the one served , yet also cause them to serve with the poor because they share in the suffering, but the focus then is on the sharing of suffering.

Poverty Mindsets are rooted in fear. Fear creeps in during a time of lack, rooted with it the lie that there will never be enough and that they must store up treasures on earth for themselves, another act of self-protection. While poverty can be generational, the mindset can be found even among the wealthy and is not a Kingdom mindset. To me, poverty is a mindset, not a state of being. A person can have a Kingdom mindset, living from Kingdom contentment, and have no earthly wealth, and a person with wealth can have a poverty mindset. Break the mindset and watch your bloodline change! Look at Chapter 3 for steps to finding the root and removing it from your life, then follow the steps found there for continued mind renewal.

In the name of Jesus Christ, I renounce poverty and fear. I break them off of my life and my bloodline.

I renounce the fear of not having enough or that there is not enough love to go around. I renounce the fear of starvation and homelessness. I renounce the fear that if I give or share what I have there won't be enough for me. I break all of these curses off of me and my bloodline and command all demons to leave now!

Father, I choose to believe that You are good and faithful. I will remember the testimonies of Your goodness and lean on them and not my own understanding. Whether I have little or plenty, I ask that you help me to be content. I bless my finances to be fruitful for the Kingdom and supply all of my family's needs. Help me to see the needs of others and meet them by Your grace and for Your glory. In Jesus name, amen.

Use the following identity statements and scriptures to help you speak truth over yourself whenever thoughts come your way.

Identity Statements

I am a new creation in Christ; I was made to love others.
I honor others for who they are in Christ.
I am not a victim; I am victorious in Christ.
I am the light of the world; I share Christ by my love.
I love because He first loved.
God has never failed, He provides all my needs.

I can be content in all things; my contentment comes from Christ, not circumstances.
I am generous and will prosper.
I have no fear of lack because I rest in Jehovah Jireh; God is my provision.

Scripture

But thanks be to God! He gives us the victory through our Lord Jesus Christ.
1 Corinthians 15:57 NIV

Repent of this wickedness and pray to the Lord in the hope that he may forgive you for having such a thought in your heart. For I see that you are full of bitterness and captive to sin.
Acts 8:22-23 NIV

And when you stand praying, if you hold anything against anyone, forgive them, so that your Father in heaven may forgive you your sins.
Mark 11:25 NIV

Do not say, "I'll pay you back for this wrong!"
Wait for the Lord, and he will avenge you.
Proverbs 20:22 NIV

Do not repay anyone evil for evil. Be careful to do what is right in the eyes of everyone. If it is possible, as far as it depends on you, live at peace with everyone. Do not take revenge, my dear friends, but leave room for God's wrath, for it is written: "It is mine to avenge; I will repay," says the Lord. On the contrary:

"If your enemy is hungry, feed him;
*   if he is thirsty, give him something to drink.*
In doing this, you will heap burning coals on his head."

Do not be overcome by evil, but overcome evil with good.
Romans 12:17-21

A heart at peace gives life to the body, but envy rots the
bones.
Proverbs 14:30 NIV

Do nothing out of selfish ambition or vain conceit.
Rather, in humility value others above yourselves,
Philippians 2:3 NIV

I was young and now I am old, yet I have never seen the
righteous forsaken or their children begging bread.
Psalm 37:25 NIV

Better the poor whose walk is blameless than the rich
whose ways are perverse.
Proverbs 28:6 NIV

A generous person will prosper; whoever refreshes
others will be refreshed.
Proverbs 11:25 NIV

And my God will meet all your needs according to the
riches of his glory in Christ Jesus.
Philippians 4:19 NIV

Mind Renewal Example

The temptation to want revenge for offenses comes to mind, declare, "I have forgiven and released _____ (name) from all offenses. I will not live in the bondage of bitterness, I will not overcome evil with evil, but will overcome by good. (*Romans 12:17-21*)

OR

The thought that you will not have enough comes to mind, you fight back with, "It is a lie of the enemy that I live in lack; God has never failed me and He meets all of my needs."

Activation

1. After following the steps in Chapter Three, ask God how He would like you to serve others. Listen for His answer and take steps to do that.

2. Handwrite two notes of encouragement and give them or mail them to people who usually encourage you or that you look up to.

3. Ask the Lord if there are any areas where you need to increase your generosity. Follow His leading and watch how He brings peace over you.

◆ ◆ ◆

8. TAKING A STAND AGAINST ANXIETY AND FEAR

Do not let your hearts be troubled. You believe in God;
believe also in me.
John 14:1 NIV

Anxiety has become so prevalent in our society that it is expected for someone to have it; you can hardly have a conversation without hearing the words "my anxiety." Anxiety is fear wrapped up in a nervous response. Anxiety causes thoughts of "what if" to spiral into imaginations of the worst possible outcomes. For some, panic sets in at that moment and creates a panic attack. The fear of an imagined danger causes a fight or flight response and steals the breath of the individual. Years of secular counseling rarely help with anything more than coping mechanisms, because it is spiritual at its root.

The demons behind anxiety often come in through abuse and manipulation. Deliverance is typically needed first, and should be followed up with allowing God to bring healing to the initial root of the trauma, then continually renewing the mind. I am not negating the reality of medically caused anxiety, though I do believe even many chronic health issues can be linked to trauma. For instance, doctors know that sexual abuse during childhood is related to IBS as an adult. When asked if I think something has a spiritual root or is solely a health issue, I respond that there is no harm in exploring the spiritual side through deliverance, emotional healing, and prayer, and the only way to find out is to try. If you heard of a treatment for a chronic disease that was risk-free, relatively quick, often free, and had many testimonies of success, wouldn't you want to try it?

I want to speak directly to those afflicted with anxiety and fear:

Anxiety can look different for each person so we will not go into the specific thoughts, but most individuals already know if they struggle with anxiety and if their thoughts jump to the worst-case scenarios sending fear through their body. If that is you, know that there is hope and freedom. Do not allow the lies of the enemy to make you think you are stuck forever. I have walked many people through deliverance who are now free of anxiety, off of medications, and living lives of peace, however, it took effort and persistence on their part. It is so important to recognize the anxious thoughts before they grow and to cast them down immediately.

Another important thing to mention: your words matter, and your view of anxiety matters. You must lose ownership of it and not claim it as your own any longer. "My anxiety" should not be a part of a believer's vocabulary. You do not have it, you are struggling with it, and our struggle is not with flesh and blood, so neither are our weapons. It is not the badge of honor that it has been made out to be, but neither is there shame in it. These mindsets must be broken for you to stand up in great authority against the tactics of the enemy that have bound you up.

In the name of Jesus Christ, I stand against the enemy that has placed anxiety in my life and I cut you off! I renounce all anxiety and fear. I renounce the spiraling thoughts of "what if" and panic attacks. I renounce the false imaginations of the worst outcomes and every lie spoken about my identity when they happen. I cut off every demon behind anxiety and break your curses off of me and my bloodline. I command every demon to leave and go to the pit now!

I command every cellular structure in my mind to come into alignment with the Kingdom of Heaven. Mind be healed, emotions be healed, hormones and chemicals come into balance now. I bless my imagination to be at peace and sanctified. Anxiety leave now, in Jesus' name!

Father, I thank you that you have given me a sound mind. I thank You that I can find peace in You, that You are my shield and my covering. I thank you that I do not need to fear the terror by night or the arrows by day. I will fear no evil because You are with me. I ask that You bring complete healing over my mind, body, and emotions. Thank you that I can go to Your throne of grace and receive healing. In the name of Jesus, amen.

Fear

Fear also includes a wide scope of thoughts, but is often more specific than anxiety. There are over 500 named phobias, and probably more that are less common. Fear also plays tricks on the imagination to make something bigger, scarier, or closer than it is. There is a natural fear that causes us to be cautious when crossing a street or when handling a potentially dangerous situation, but there is also a fear that comes in people even when danger is not present. For instance, a person can have a healthy respect and know to be cautious around blood, but there is a fear of blood that can cause a person to react even when no blood is present or from a distance. The latter is the fear we want to break.

Many people have a fear of being home alone, a fear of the dark, a fear of death, or a fear of the future, just to name a few common ones. These fears creep in and hold individuals back from living life to its fullest, or at the very least, cause torment in the mind. Many other fears are rooted in the subjects from the previous chapters, such as the fear of abandonment. In those cases, first work through those mindsets and behaviors, then if the fear is still there, search for the root of fear using the tools in Chapter 3.

But first, let's break the curse of fear, and declare the following:

In the name of Jesus Christ, I cut off every spirit of fear that has tried to steal my destiny. I renounce fear and giving in to the tactics of fear. I especially renounce the fear of _____ (name every fear you know you struggle against), and I renounce the lies associated with it. I renounce every curse of fear and break those curses off of me and my bloodline. I command every demon of fear to leave me now and go to the pit!

Father, I thank You that You have not given me a spirit of fear, but of power, love, and a sound mind. I ask that You fill me with complete peace and help me to comprehend the great authority and power

I walk in by Your Spirit. I repent for trusting in fear over Your word , which declares You have good things in store for me. I agree with You that You had a destiny for me before the Earth was formed. I ask that You further fill me to overflow and that Your peace will not only flow to me, but to those around me. In Jesus' name, amen

Identity Statements

If this doesn't go well, I will be okay because I have Christ in me.
God works all things together for my good.
I do not have a spirit of fear.
I have the mind of Christ, a sound mind!
I will not live in chaos; peace is my inheritance.
The Spirit of the God of Comfort lives in me.
I will not be afraid or discouraged, the Lord my God is with me.

Scripture

May the God of hope fill you with all joy and peace as you trust in him, so that you may overflow with hope by the power of the Holy Spirit.
Romans 15:13 NIV

So we say with confidence, "The Lord is my helper; I will not be afraid. What can mere mortals do to me?
Hebrews 13:6 NIV

Do not be anxious about anything, but in every situation, by prayer and petition, with thanksgiving, present your requests to God. And the peace of God, which transcends all understanding, will guard your hearts and your minds in Christ Jesus.
Philippians 4:6-7 NIV

So do not fear, for I am with you; do not be dismayed, for I am your God. I will strengthen you and help you; I will uphold you with my righteous right hand.
Isaiah 41:10 NIV

Be strong and courageous. Do not be afraid or terrified because of them, for the Lord your God goes with you; he will never leave you nor forsake you.
Deuteronomy 31:6 NIV

For God has not given us a spirit of fear, but of power and of love and of a sound mind.
2 Timothy 1:7 NKJV

The Lord is my shepherd, I lack nothing.
He makes me lie down in green pastures,
he leads me beside quiet waters,
he refreshes my soul.
He guides me along the right paths
for his name's sake.
Even though I walk
through the darkest valley,
I will fear no evil,
for you are with me;
your rod and your staff,

they comfort me.
You prepare a table before me
   in the presence of my enemies.
You anoint my head with oil;
   my cup overflows.
Surely your goodness and love will follow me
   all the days of my life,
and I will dwell in the house of the Lord
   forever.
Psalm 23 NIV

The Lord is my light and my salvation— whom shall I fear? The Lord is the stronghold of my life— of whom shall I be afraid?
Psalm 27:1 NIV

Mind Renewal Example

When thoughts of fear try to take hold, respond with, "I will not give in to fear. I am strong and courageous, and I am victorious in Christ!"

OR

When the thoughts of anxiety come, tell them, "The Lord is my light and my salvation— whom shall I fear? The Lord is the stronghold of my life— of whom shall I be afraid?" (Psalm 27:1)

Activation

1. After following the steps in Chapter 3 to find the root of the fear, identify if or where that has caused you to shy away from the call of God on your life. Now take a step towards that call, even if fear and intimidation are felt in the moment (ex: a fear of rejection could have caused you to not flag during worship like you have felt led to. After breaking rejection and fear, pick up a flag and worship freely).

2. Identify if there is a location in your home or car where thoughts of anxiety come on the most. If there is, bless the area, command spirits of fear to leave, invite the presence of God to come in and fill that space, and then place notes with the scriptures and identity statements around the area.

♦ ♦ ♦

9. WIPING OUT SHAME

Therefore, there is now no condemnation for those who are in Christ Jesus, because through Christ Jesus the law of the Spirit who gives life has set you free from the law of sin and death.
Romans 8:1-2 NIV

Dirty Little Secrets

Shame seeks to separate believers from the family of faith by telling them they are no good, dirty, and can never be free or clean from what they have done or what they have thought. Shame knows that if it can keep someone quiet, they will forever be bound up in secrecy and regret, and never able to reach their fullest potential. Shame partners with worthlessness to tell people that they cannot be loved because of their sins.

The truth is, that Christ died to set us free from

death and shame. His blood fully cleanses us of all iniquity and guilt. We just have to receive what He has already done. Shame keeps people in cycles of sin by telling them that there is no hope because of what they have done. It also tells many that they will be rejected if they tell anyone the truth. Freedom is found in opening up and revealing the pain we have hidden.

It is important to have trustworthy wise counsel in your life whom you can go to to talk about anything, especially if you are in any form of leadership. We have all watched too many leaders in the Body fall publicly because what they perceived as shameful thoughts led to shameful actions. I often wonder, if they had someone they could have opened up to when the thoughts first began, could they have received deliverance and freedom from the torment and shame stopping the shame from protecting the demonic thoughts that grew into actions?

Shame of the past also seeks to put a ceiling over believers to keep them from attempting to walk in their call. When the dreams and visions of their call come to mind they say, "Who am I to do this, I am just a sinner saved by grace." The statement "I am a sinner saved by grace" is a fantastic twisting of scripture, as we know, Satan loves to twist the Word of God so closely to the truth it sounds right, but it is false and limiting. The truth is, you once *were* a sinner (see Romans 5:8), and now you are called, righteous, holy, a royal priest, a child of God, a saint, and forgiven. Walk out of your past and into your freedom and inheritance as a child of God with great authority. We can choose to look at our past with shame or as a beautiful testimony of God's goodness.

Let us break shame now.

In the name of Jesus Christ, I break the power of shame over my life! I break the fears and limitations it has placed on me. I break every lie of shame I have believed. I declare that my sin has been removed from me as far as the East is from the West. I break every curse of shame off of me and my bloodline now and command every demon behind it to leave and go to the pit, now!

Identity Statements

I set my mind on heavenly things.
I have been forgiven and set free.
I am not the sum of my mistakes, I am a new creation in Christ.
I have been crucified with Christ, it is no longer I who lives, sin has been broken.
I am washed clean by the blood of Jesus, all shame has been removed.
It is no longer I who live, but Christ who lives in me.

Scripture

But you are a chosen people, a royal priesthood, a holy nation, God's special possession, that you may declare the praises of him who called you out of darkness into his wonderful light.
1 Peter 2:9 NIV

As far as the East is from the West, so far has he removed our transgressions from us.
Psalm 103:12

Both the one who makes people holy and those who are made holy are of the same family. So Jesus is not ashamed to call them brothers and sisters.
Hebrews 2:11

fixing our eyes on Jesus, the pioneer and perfecter of faith. For the joy set before him, he endured the cross, scorning its shame, and sat down at the right hand of the throne of God.
Hebrews 12:2

Therefore, there is now no condemnation for those who are in Christ Jesus, because through Christ Jesus the law of the Spirit who gives life has set you free from the law of sin and death.
Romans 8:1-2

As it is written: "See, I lay in Zion a stone that causes people to stumble and a rock that makes them fall, and the one who believes in him will never be put to shame."
Romans 9:33

As Scripture says, "Anyone who believes in him will

never be put to shame."
Romans 10:11

Rather, <u>we have renounced secret and shameful ways;</u>
we do not use deception, nor do we distort the word of
God. On the contrary, by setting forth the truth plainly
we commend ourselves to everyone's conscience in the
sight of God.
2 Corinthians 4:2

For we know that our old self was crucified with him
so that the body ruled by sin might be done away with,
that we should no longer be slaves to sin— because
anyone who has died has been set free from sin.

Now if we died with Christ, we believe that we will also
live with him. For we know that since Christ was raised
from the dead, he cannot die again; death no longer has
mastery over him. The death he died, he died to sin once
for all; but the life he lives, he lives to God.
In the same way, count yourselves dead to sin but alive
to God in Christ Jesus. Therefore do not let sin reign in
your mortal body so that you obey its evil desires. Do
not offer any part of yourself to sin as an instrument
of wickedness, but rather offer yourselves to God as
those who have been brought from death to life, and
offer every part of yourself to him as an instrument of
righteousness. For sin shall no longer be your master,
because you are not under the law, but under grace.
Romans 6:6-18 NIV

Mind Renewal Example

When thoughts of shame come at you, simply state, "I no longer live in sin and shame, I was crucified with Christ, it is now Christ who lives in me.

OR

"I will not partner with shame, the Word of God declares, there is now no condemnation for those who are in Christ Jesus and I agree with this truth." (Romans 8:1-2)

Activation

1. Find a trustworthy mentor and break the power of shame by sharing with them the acts or thoughts that have bound you up. If there is ongoing sin, ask them to hold you accountable and check in with you.

◆ ◆ ◆

10. FINDING SWEET SLEEP

When you lie down, you will not be afraid; when you lie down, your sleep will be sweet.
Proverbs 3:24 NIV

A Window Into the Spiritual

Dreams and nightmares can reveal a lot about what is going on in our minds, our souls, and the world around us. Many hopes and dreams can be revealed, and so can schemes of the enemy in the area, torment, fear, and generational curses. Some of this is God revealing to us what we need to be aware of and others are pointing to areas we need freedom.

We have the authority over our dream life. In the story that I mentioned in Chapter One, God spoke to me and said, "You have been given authority. You can command even bad dreams to go away in the name of Jesus and they will stop." I have taught each of my children this from a young age and it worked each time to end the nightly torment. However, this was before learning about deliverance and breaking generational curses.

Who is showing up in dreams and nightmares matters. If you suffer from nightmares, take note of the demonic entities or relationships that have been shown in them. This can be a clue to what curses may still be on your bloodline. While any demon could appear in this way, the most common ones people have reported seeing in their dreams are Python, Leviathan, Satan, Baal, Molech, Jezebel, and witches. If an entity has been appearing in your nightmares, it is to be renounced, its curses broken and then commanded to leave you and your bloodline.

If a relationship is present in the nightmares, it may be a sign of an unhealthy soul tie. If it is someone from the past, break the soul tie and command any demon associated with them to leave. If the relationship is still present, you will need to pray and ask God for revelation on the health of the relationship and if an unhealthy soul tie has been formed. Break any unhealthy ties using the steps in Chapter Three.

If a relative is in nightmares, especially recurring ones, a curse may have come through that part of your ancestry. You must not accuse or condemn a person based on dreams as the enemy could also use them to attempt to destroy a relationship. I have heard many stories of nightmares with the grandmother or grandfather trying to attack the person, or recurring nightmares taking place in a specific family member's home. It never fails that a generational curse has come from that part of the family. We break the curses off the bloodline and expel the demons associated with it.

Nightmares and dreams of a sexual nature are signs of a spirit such as Lust, Jezebel, or Lilith. Again, there is no shame in recognizing it and breaking free so your future bloodline is not tormented by the same demons. When a perverse dream has physical feelings with it, often, Incubus or Succubus are present. If there are frequent sexual dreams with the same person, a soul bond needs to be broken.

In the name of Jesus Christ, I renounce the demons that afflict me at night. I revoke all power and authority that I or my ancestors gave you. I renounce all demons including but not limited to; Python, Leviathan, Satan, Baal, Molech, Witchcraft, Jezebel, Lust, Lilith, Incubus, and Succubus. I break your curses off of me and my bloodline now and command every demon to leave and go to the pit now!

What we allow in our lives can affect our dream life. When we watch violent or perverse video games, movies, social media, books, magazines, etc. we open doors for the enemy to torment us and play games with our dream life and imagination. Our eyes are the window to our body, and what we watch affects the health of our soul. We have to recognize that we are not of this world and cannot partner with the demonic just because it is what everyone else is doing. We are called to be set apart, holy, and consecrated.

In the name of Jesus, I renounce watching movies, shows, & clips that allow demonic influence to my mind, my eyes, my ears, and my dreams. I renounce playing evil video games and fantasy role-playing games and the effect they have had on my mind. I renounce reading inappropriate books, magazines, and blogs and all the effects they have had on my dreams and imagination. I renounce all fantasizing and ungodly daydreaming that has allowed the enemy to play freely in my mind. I break all curses related to these things from me and my bloodline and I command every demon associated to leave now!

Sweet Sleep

Most people experience sweet, peaceful sleep after going through deliverance and finding full freedom. A small minority, however, either still have to wage war against the demonic to find freedom in their sleep, or they may need greater levels of freedom. For a few people, it takes several sessions to gain freedom, depending on their history.

Now that the curses have been broken, soul ties cut, and the tools to walk boldly in your identity have been given, it is time to wield them well. Rather than waiting for the nightmares, before bed each night, make declarations and pray for the Lord of Heaven's Armies to guard your rest.

Declarations and Prayer

I declare that in peace I will lie down and sleep.
I declare that the Lord is my salvation, of whom shall I be afraid.
I declare that my sleep will be sweet.

Father, I thank you for the freedom you have brought me and my bloodline. I ask that you guard my rest tonight so that I can sleep peacefully in the shadow of the Almighty without fear or dread of the enemy. I ask that You purify my dreamlife so I can perceive Your will and hear from You in my rest. I bless my family to be at peace as the shalom of Heaven settles in our home. In Jesus' name, Amen.

Scripture
Also, see the scriptures in Chapter Nine

In peace I will lie down and sleep, for you alone, Lord, make me dwell in safety.

Psalm 4:8 NIV

Whoever dwells in the shelter of the Most High will rest in the shadow of the Almighty.
Psalm 91:1 NIV

The Lord will keep you from all harm, he will watch over your life; the Lord will watch over your coming and going both now and forevermore.
Psalm 121:7-8 NIV

When you lie down, you will not be afraid; when you lie down, your sleep will be sweet.
Proverbs 3:24 NIV

No weapon forged against you will prevail, and you will refute every tongue that accuses you. This is the heritage of the servants of the Lord, and this is their vindication from me,"
declares the Lord.
Isaiah 54:17 NIV

"The eye is the lamp* of the body. If your eyes are healthy, your whole body will be full of light. But if your eyes are unhealthy, your whole body will be full of darkness. If then the light within you is darkness, how great is that darkness!
No one can serve two masters. Either you will hate the one and love the other, or you will be devoted to the one and despise the other. You cannot serve both God and money."
Matthew 6:22-24 NIV
*Some translations use window

And the peace of God, which transcends all understanding, will guard your hearts and your minds in Christ Jesus.
Philippians 4:7 NIV

Activation

1. Take time to pray over your bedroom and the rooms of your children. Bless the rooms to be filled with the peace of Heaven. Repent of any unholy acts that took place there. Command any unholy spirits to leave.

2. As you walk around your house, pray and ask God if there is anything in your house that needs to go. He may reveal an uneasy feeling about certain items you have purchased or gifts. If you are not certain, ask a mentor to pray about an item with you and allow the Holy Spirit to reveal any darkness hidden behind it. (EX: Someone I know was given a hanging decoration that they did not realize was a third eye.)

◆ ◆ ◆

11. WALKING
IN POWER

His divine power has given us everything we need for a godly life through our knowledge of him who called us by his own glory and goodness. Through these he has given us his very great and precious promises, so that through them you may participate in the divine nature, having escaped the corruption in the world caused by evil desires.

For this very reason, make every effort to add to your faith goodness; and to goodness, knowledge; and to knowledge, self-control; and to self-control, perseverance; and to perseverance, godliness; and to godliness, mutual affection; and to mutual affection, love. For if you possess these qualities in increasing measure, they will keep you from being ineffective and unproductive in your knowledge of our Lord Jesus Christ.
2 Peter 1:3-8 NIV

Finally, 2 Peter 1:3-8 leaves us with great instructions for ongoing maturity as He who began a great work in us will continue to work in us to produce an image that looks more and more like Christ each day so long as we desire to be more like Him. We walk through the process of deliverance and emotional healing to cleanse us of the things that would try to hold us back. This leads to individuals walking more in the fruit of the Spirit as they yield to Holy Spirit and tune in more closely, no longer battling the internal thoughts and emotions but being restored to the fullness of peace that Christ offers.

Many more bloodline curses should be addressed through deliverance. My goal for this book is to help individuals take steps toward finding inner and emotional healing from home, which requires touching on the subject of deliverance. There is far more to it! A good starting point is Mike Brewers's Self Deliverance Guide: A step-by-step guide to freedom from bondage and closing of spiritual doors. I do, however, recommend finding someone trained in bloodline deliverance to take you through a full session, this is especially important if you or anyone in your ancestry was involved in the occult including witchcraft, new age, reiki, Freemasonry, secret societies, satanism, or other false religions.

After deliverance and inner healing, it is necessary to keep our lives free from immorality (Hebrews 13, for one) and live worthy of the calling (Ephesians 4:1). The books of Luke and Matthew each speak about spirits leaving and then coming back with more wicked spirits. Once we clean out our house, it must be filled and sealed with the Holy Spirit, no longer leaving open doors for any wicked thing to enter. Guard your heart above all else and keep watch over what you allow in your life and home being careful not to welcome evil into your life.

Use the tools in this book as often as you need to. I also highly suggest you read the following identity statements out loud each morning for three weeks. It takes three weeks to form a habit. Dedicating two minutes each morning to focusing your thoughts on God and your true identity will kickstart renewing your mind. Each of these identity statements is directly from scripture and hopefully will show you how you can wield the Word of God over yourself to strengthen your identity in Christ.

Identity Statement

I receive my inheritance as a child of the King! I get to partner and co-labor with Christ and the body of Christ.

I have given my life as an offering to Christ; it is no longer I who live but He who lives in me! We are united, He in me and I in Him!
I have been united with Christ even in His death,

burial, and resurrection. I was raised with Him, therefore, death no longer has a hold on me.

God raised me with Christ and seated me with him in the heavenly realms in Christ Jesus, above all rule, all power, all authority, and above every name that is named, not only in this age but also in the one to come.

I carry the authority of Christ. I have authority over sickness, sin, the flesh, demons, and over the world. I have been given the authority to bring the Kingdom of Heaven to Earth and to displace darkness.

I am the salt of the earth and the light of the world.

I have the full armor of God. I put on the breastplate of righteousness, the belt of truth, the helmet of salvation, the shoes of peace. I take up the shield of faith and the sword of the Spirit. For the weapons of my warfare are not fleshly. They are divinely powerful to tear down the strongholds of darkness.

I can do all things through Christ because greater is He who is in me than he who is in the world.

His divine power has given me everything I need for a godly life through my knowledge of Him who called me by his glory and goodness.

I am a chosen person, a royal priest, part of a holy nation, God's special possession, so that I may declare the praises of Him who called me out of darkness into His wonderful light.

(Inspired by The Biblical Guidebook to Deliverance by Dr. Randy Clark)

Scripture on Continuing in Holiness

Are you so foolish? After beginning by means of the Spirit, are you now trying to finish by means of the flesh?
Galatians 3:3 NIV

Instead, speaking the truth in love, we will grow to become in every respect the mature body of him who is the head, that is, Christ. From him the whole body, joined and held together by every supporting ligament, grows and builds itself up in love, as each part does its work.
Ephesians 4:15-16 NIV

As for other matters, brothers and sisters, we instructed you how to live in order to please God, as in fact you are living. Now we ask you and urge you in the Lord Jesus to do this more and more. For you know what instructions we gave you by the authority of the Lord Jesus.

It is God's will that you should be sanctified: that you should avoid sexual immorality; that each of you should learn to control your own body in a way that is holy and honorable, not in passionate lust like the pagans, who do not know God; and that in this matter no one should wrong or take advantage of a brother or

sister. The Lord will punish all those who commit such sins, as we told you and warned you before. For God did not call us to be impure, but to live a holy life. Therefore, anyone who rejects this instruction does not reject a human being but God, the very God who gives you his Holy Spirit.
1 Thessalonians 4:1-8 NIV

Being confident of this, that he who began a good work in you will carry it on to completion until the day of Christ Jesus.
Philippians 1:6 NIV

Therefore, my dear friends, as you have always obeyed —not only in my presence, but now much more in my absence, continue to work out your salvation with fear and trembling, for it is God who works in you to will and to act in order to fulfill his good purpose.

Do everything without grumbling or arguing, so that you may become blameless and pure, "children of God without fault in a warped and crooked generation." Then you will shine among them like stars in the sky as you hold firmly to the word of life. And then I will be able to boast on the day of Christ that I did not run or labor in vain.
Philippians 2:12-16 NIV

Since, then, you have been raised with Christ, set your hearts on things above, where Christ is, seated at the right hand of God. Set your minds on things above, not on earthly things. For you died, and your life is now hidden with Christ in God. When Christ, who is your life, appears, then you also will appear with him in glory.

Put to death, therefore, whatever belongs to your earthly nature: sexual immorality, impurity, lust, evil desires and greed, which is idolatry.
Colossians 3:1-5 NIV

Therefore, brothers and sisters, since we have confidence to enter the Most Holy Place by the blood of Jesus, by a new and living way opened for us through the curtain, that is, his body, and since we have a great priest over the house of God, let us draw near to God with a sincere heart and with the full assurance that faith brings, having our hearts sprinkled to cleanse us from a guilty conscience and having our bodies washed with pure water. Let us hold unswervingly to the hope we profess, for he who promised is faithful. And let us consider how we may spur one another on toward love and good deeds, not giving up meeting together, as some are in the habit of doing, but encouraging one another —and all the more as you see the Day approaching.

If we deliberately keep on sinning after we have received the knowledge of the truth, no sacrifice for sins is left, but only a fearful expectation of judgment and of raging fire that will consume the enemies of God.
Hebrews 10:19-27 NIV

Make every effort to live in peace with everyone and to be holy; without holiness no one will see the Lord. 15 See to it that no one falls short of the grace of God and that no bitter root grows up to cause trouble and defile many.

16 See that no one is sexually immoral, or is godless like Esau, who for a single meal sold his inheritance rights as the oldest son.
Hebrews 12:14-16

A FINAL NOTE

Finding the Root Example

The following is an example of how a time of prayer to uncover the root pain may play out. It will be different for each person.

Step 1 I decide I want to work on breaking fear off of my life today. I find a quiet place and turn my attention to God.

Step 2 I ask, "Holy Spirit, where did the fear first get in?" He began to show me a childhood memory where I felt out of control and fearful of what would happen next.

Step 3 I renounce the trauma of the moment, break the unhealthy soul ties with the person who made me feel scared, and forgive the offender. .Then I ask God, "What lie did I begin believing in this moment?" He reveals that I believed that I felt unprotected and alone.

Step 4 I Renounce the lies and ask God, "Father, what is the truth?" He reveals that He is my protector and was even protecting me in that moment. I ask, "What do You want me to know about that moment?" He reveals the spiritual atmosphere that was around me and that I was responding to that and not the individual. I begin to have peace fill me as the revelation of truth comes into my life. I asked Him, "Is there anything else You would like me to know?" He reveals His love for me as a daughter.

Step 5 I receive the truth and declare "I declare that God is my protector, of whom shall I fear? I cut all ties with fear and I tear down the strongholds of fear the enemy has placed in my mind. I choose to believe His truth about my identity as a daughter of the Most High King.

I hope this example allows you to see how easy it can be to allow God to work through the pain we have buried by getting to the root issue and speaking the truth about it. This is a very generic example because I want you to hear from God for yourself to receive the truth of His word.

I pray that as you walk through these tools you find an abundance of healing and joy. I also hope that as you are equipped you can pass these tools on through your family line so you leave behind an inheritance of freedom.

Blessings in Christ,
Cherish

Resources

Brewer, Mike Self-Deliverance Guide: A step-by-step guide to freedom from bondage and closing of spiritual doors 2022

Clark, Randy The Biblical Guidebook to Deliverance 2015

Holy Bible: New International Version. Zondervan, 2005

Find a believer trained in bloodline deliverance: Thewellglobal.life

Discover more about the Kingdom that is here and now!

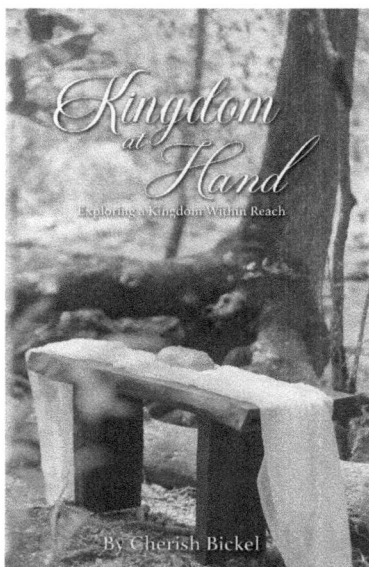

Available on Amazon, Kindle and at TheBickel.com

Want to know more about
what we do? Find us at:

TheBickel.com